The Cursed Land of Lustful Women
and
The Power of Storytelling

The Cursed Land of Lustful Women
and
The Power of Storytelling
(Performance Text with Notes)

Kanika Gupta

Kaveri Books
New Delhi - 110002

SLOVENE ETHNOGRAPHIC MUSEUM

The Cursed Land of Lustful Women and
The Power of Storytelling
(Performance Text with Notes)

By
Kanika Gupta

ISBN : 978-93-86463-23-4
First Published in 2023

The performance was produced as part of the residency for the project Taking Care. Ethnographic and World Cultures Museums as Spaces of Care (2019-2023), which was co-funded by the Creative Europe Programme of the European Union.

The project has been supported by

takingcare

Co-funded by the Creative Europe Programme of the European Union

Published by

Kaveri Books
4832/24, Ansari Road, Darya Ganj
New Delhi - 110 002 (India)
Ph. : +91 11 23288140, 4707 2321
E-mail : kaveribooks@gmail.com & info@kaveribooks.com
Website : www.kaveribooks.com

Co-published by

SLOVENE ETHNOGRAPHIC MUSEUM
Metelkova ulica 2, 1000
Ljubljana, Slovenia

Typesetting at Creative Graphics, Delhi

PRINTED IN INDIA

Dedicated

to

Phoolan Devi

(1963 – 2001)

Who was beaten unconscious for wanting to save an old Neem tree, her inheritance.

Acknowledgements

This performance text is a result of years of pondering over history, the stories embedded in history, issues of identity and my own self. Its process consists of a lot of internal work and even more external work which was laborious and took more years than expected.

As a Kathak dancer I was taught to perform on religious themes and stories I did not personally relate to and I always searched for a story to tell which I could truly identify with. I searched for many years, and it was only during the research work for my Ph.D. thesis that I was able to go through a huge amount of ancient Indian literature and create my own stories out of it.

The process has been so long that it is impossible to be able to acknowledge each one who has been part of it and has helped in some way. However, most importantly, I would like to thank the Slovene Ethnographic Museum, Ljubljana, and Taking Care project which provided the necessary funding for the creation of the performance. Tina Palaić and Ralf Čeplak Mencin have been instrumental in the realisation of this project. My dear friend, Tatjana Marušič, has always made me feel at home in Ljubljana. Ljubljana is a hundred times more beautiful to me because of her. Magda Reja has showered me with her affections and Mojca Račič has been extremely kind in welcoming me so lovingly.

Aljosa Kutnjac has constantly supported me in my endeavours; I was lucky to find friends like Lucka Lesnic and Ana Jelnikar. Several other friends in Slovenia have given me immense love and support.

Arghyadeep Roy was kind enough to understand my ideas and has beautifully shot the trailer of the performance. Sneha Agarwala from Kolkata, Vankar Mukesh and Nilesh Shekha from Bhujodi helped me in sourcing my costume.

Saket Prakash has always been there in hard times, and he supported me when I had nowhere else to go. Several other friends extended support including Bobby John, Devas Dixit, Raja Anand, Ravi Shankar, Akash Kumar Sahu, Sushil Kumar and Yogesh Mallinathpur. A special thanks to Shrey Prakash and Tanmoy Howlader who went out of their way to help this project.

I thank my parents and brother for partially funding the initial phase of the project. Lastly, I am truly grateful to Abhishek and the entire team of Kaveri Books for making this publication come true.

The entire staff of the Slovene Ethnographic Museum has wholeheartedly supported me and showered me with their affections. I truly love you all.

My work and Art History is dedicated to my teacher Professor Deepak Kannal and I thank him for his feedback and suggestions on this performance. He introduced me to the pleasures of Gāthāsaptasati.

I am indebted to all the wonderful people of Slovenia for their love that I continue to receive and to all those who took their time out to watch this performance. You all made this performance; without you all it would have simply been a rehearsal.

I bow down to the trees under whose shade I could tell my stories.

May the forests and rivers of Slovenia, India and the whole world thrive till the end of Sun and Moon.

Kanika Gupta

Introduction

The Slovene Ethnographic Museum (SEM) has been actively engaged in European projects for many years, providing opportunities to situate our experiences and practices consistently within the European museum context. By doing this, we draw attention to our unique characteristics and develop our contents and methodological actions in line with them. Especially in dealing with non-European collections, SEM participates in current discussions in this area which, among other things, direct museums to share its authority and care for heritage with the communities of origin, as well as to the repatriation of museum objects. Our consideration of how to interpret non-European collections from the European periphery has been encouraged by the project Taking Care: Ethnographic and World Cultures Museums as Spaces of Care (2019–2023), which links thirteen European museums with these collections.

The project was created as a reaction to climate change, which is becoming more and more noticeable in our region, and the requirement to mitigate its effects. Its purpose is to include the participating museums in the discussion about how human activity affects the environment, and to inspire museum professionals to develop more sustainable practices for their organizations as well as for their interactions with heritage holders and their cultural heritage. Through collaboration between museum curators, researchers, activists, and artists, the project highlights ecological knowledge from non-European collections and encourages thought on more sustainable ways of living.

As part of the project, the SEM hosted Art Historian Kanika Gupta, Ph.D., from New Delhi, who spent three months in Ljubljana investigating the museum's Indian collection. At the same time, she also planned several activities for the museum's visitors to increase awareness of Indian mythology in relation to the environmental crises. We were able to view her artistic documentary film, titled '**It was in Spring**', which addressed the issue of excessive construction and its effects on both nature and people. She also challenged people to think about the importance of trees for our way of life by hosting a poetry competition called '*Peozijadreves*' in Slovene. She created a unique experience with her artistic performance '**The Cursed Land of Lustful Women**', in which she fused dance and narrative to produce an artistic piece with a strong message: we must protect nature for the welfare of people.

Valuable for SEM are not only the professional outcomes of the project itself, but also the human ties that are woven around such work and which conform to the mission of a "museum about people and for people".

Natalija Polenec
Director
Slovene Ethnographic Museum
Ljubljana, Slovenia

Mobilising Indian Storytelling Tradition as an Archive of Environmental and Cultural Knowledge

Heatwaves, fires, droughts, floods, and extreme sea level rises – all of which have a significant impact on the daily lives of the population in the affected areas and, among other things, destroy their cultural heritage – are increasingly common phenomena that we characterize as climate change. These processes cause severe food and water shortage and contribute to massive human displacement by destroying homes and livelihood. Often, once-colonised areas that have historically undergone processes of exploitation of both natural and human resources are affected, so climate phenomena contribute in particular to increasing social inequality. Additionally, climate change has an impact on wildlife habitats, the extinction of animal and plant species, soil depletion, and water pollution. The excessive exploitation of a planet, which is based on the unbridled capitalist ideology of progress and constant development, exacerbates the situation to extremes. When greed takes over, capitalism becomes an end in itself and consumption a way of life. It is becoming clear that, in order to successfully manage and mitigate its consequences, we will all have to tackle it together – by realizing the concept of degrowth, and, above all, in cooperation and solidarity.

When we think about the future of the planet, the environmental crisis intertwined with other crises (health, financial, political, media, military and others) raises and reinforces feelings of fear and anxiety. On the other hand, environmental catastrophes also encourage reflections on the responsibility of individuals, social institutions and the whole social system to mitigate their consequences, which is reflected in a number of movements and actions calling for faster and more effective action. As socially responsible institutions, museums are involved in many discussions addressing climate change. Through a variety of activities, they enable discovering and learning about past knowledge, skills and values contained in museum collections, thereby assisting in making sense of the current social situation. Museums also strive to act as safe social spaces for dialogue and the exploration of alternatives, and thus encouraging active responses to the environmental challenges.

In response to this pressing issue, thirteen European ethnographic museums have designed the project, '**Taking Care: Ethnographic and World Cultures Museums as Spaces of Care (2019-2023)**', which engages such museums in social discussions about humans' environmental impact, and possible strategies for creating a more just and sustainable future. The aim of the project is to explore non-European museum collections and ecological knowledge in them, which, with the participation of curators, researchers, activists, artists and heritage holders from the source communities, can serve as an inspiration for alternative climate change strategies. Project activities are based on the concept of care, which connects the preservation of material and intangible aspects of the heritage by strengthening cooperation with people who are connected to heritage in various ways.

As part of the project, the Slovene Ethnographic Museum invited art historian Kanika Gupta from New Delhi for a residency. In her research and artistic work, Gupta explores ancient Indian art and mythology, and links them to contemporary environmental challenges. Between July and September 2021, Gupta investigated the museum's Indian collection in this light and produced several events for the museum's audience. In addition to a literary competition, which invited original poetry on the theme of trees, the museum's visitors were able to see her documentary, '**It Was in**

Spring', which draws attention to the gentrification of New Delhi through Gupta's personal story, and her artistic performance, '**The Cursed Land of Lustful Women**', in which nature plays the most important role. Through her work, Kanika Gupta reactivated the museum's Indian collection as an archive of environmental and cultural knowledge.

The Cursed Land of Lustful Women is inspired by Indian stories from the Buddhist, Jain, and Brahmanical traditions that intertwine issues of nature and attitudes towards it with gender inequalities, as well as power relationships between various social groups. As Kanika Gupta explains in her chapter in this book, these religions have taken over many narratives of older traditions and transformed them to serve their purposes. Through her performance, she attempts to trace the ancient Indian cult of nature worship, and by doing so she inevitably creates a new narrative as a result of her selection of ancient stories and, in particular, her understanding of the past and present. The performance stems from her experience of a rapidly changing environment, which she understands as an irreparable loss, and from her desires and expectations for the future, inspired by contemporary narratives about climate change and humanity's role in these processes. Its purpose is to use the dance movements of the Indian dance tradition Kathak, accompanied by the vivid narrative of the performer, to transcend the romantic views on Indian culture and invite people to dialogue about the environmental and social crisis the performance reveals to viewers. It also seeks to invite audiences to explore the feelings and emotions that the performance provokes and ponder upon their own responsibility for a better tomorrow.

The performance tells a story from the days when profound social and environmental changes began to take place in India. Although it is full of meaning and symbolism, it is simple in its narration. Gupta uses few words as a Kathak performer to connect to the natural environment that serves as the backdrop for the performance. In doing so, she focuses on the sounds of nature, the wind, the trees, the buzzing of insects and the gentle murmur of the night, which represent music instead of recorded sounds. In the performance we see many movements, which Gupta performs in silence, full of feelings and aesthetic pleasure. The importance of performance is not only in what it tells us at the level of a story and what it allows us to feel along with it, but above all in what it allows us to think – and these are different aspects of climate and social justice.

During her residency, Kanika Gupta performed the piece eleven times, two of which were public rehearsals, three were organized by the Slovene Ethnographic Museum, and one was recorded by the Museum for documentary and archival purposes. The performance recording is now available on the museum's website and YouTube channel, making the artwork permanently accessible. Gupta gave some performances in various parts of Slovenia, broadening her audience.

The performance received very positive feedback. It moved the audience and piqued their interest in what was behind the narratives, what their historical context was, and how the piece related to current events. This booklet has emerged precisely in order to outline the context of collaboration with Kanika Gupta and to present the starting points of this performance and Kanika's reflections of the current situation through it. We wish you a pleasant reading experience!

Tina Palaić

Curator

Project Taking Care: Ethnographic and World Cultures Museums as Spaces of Care

Slovene Ethnographic Museum

Ljubljana, Slovenia

Characters and Place Names in the Performance

Brahmadatta	=	An ancient Indian king
Vārāṇasi	=	An ancient Indian city
Kosala	=	An ancient Indian kingdom
Princess Kaṇhā	=	A princess in ancient Indian myths, also known as Draupadi
King Pāṇḍu	=	A king in ancient Indian myths
The five sons of King Pāṇḍu		
Goddess Uṣā	=	The Vedic goddess of dawn

1

Connecting the Dots: Performances and Poetry

The female and the tree, known by various names in visual art traditions of India is arguably the most popular motif in Indian art since ancient times.

Fig. 1 : Performance at Križ near Sežana, Tončinova domačija – Majda Škrlj, Slovenia. Hosted by Mojca Račič and Majda Škrlj, 25 September 202. Credit: Mojca Račič

Fig. 2 : The female and tree motif; holding the branch of a tree like the innumerable yakṣī in Indian art. During performance shoot at Tivoli Park, Ljubljana, Slovenia. Credit: Nadja Valentinčič Furlan

Fig. 3 : Mahākokā devatā, Bharhut. Credit - Kirit Mankodi and US Department of Homeland Security

Fig. 4 : The female and tree, Bharhut. Credit - Indian Museum Kolkata

Yakṣī, śālabhañjikā, śālastrī are a few terms used to describe this idea. This motif and the cult of *yakṣī* has been the subject of my Ph.D. thesis (Gupta 2022) and took root a long time ago.

The splendour of trees and forests has been remarkably captured in Indian art and it often left me wondering if the beauty depicted could really exist. From Mahākokādevatā (Kannal, Gupta 2019) (Fig. 3) of Bharhut to Kakubha rāgini of Bundi (Fig. 5) the magic of this motif is ceaseless.

Fig. 5 : Kakubha Rāgini, amid enchanting trees.
Credit: Victoria and Albert Museum, London, no. IM.43.1933

I have tried to delve into the mysteries of this motif in my thesis and hope to publish it someday. For now, it must be stated that I wished to create a performance with trees since long and it would have never happened if I had not worked on the female and tree motif for my Ph.D.

This performance is this motif, of female and tree, in which both the tree and its female manifestation tell their stories. There is also a reference to a wish-fulfilling tree (kalpavṛkṣa) which one often comes across in ancient Indian art (see fig 8, 9) and literature. Ancient myths say that plants and trees were once capable of fulfilling all human desires, including precious stone and gold jwellery. This motif is profusely depicted in the sculpture of Bharhut (see fig. 10-21).

Fig. 6-7 : During a rehearsal, Ljubljana, Slovenia. Credit: Tina Palaić

Fig. 8 : Wish fulfilling tree, Vidisha. Photographer - Beglar, Joseph David, photographed in 1875. Credit: British Library

Fig. 9 : Wish Fulfilling Tree, Vidisha. Photographed in 2022. Credit: Indian Museum, Kolkata No. 1795, Tanmoy Howlader

Fig. 10 : Trees and foliage sprouting ornaments and depictions of Jātaka stories, Bharhut. Credit: Indian Museum, Kolkata

Fig. 11 : Trees and foliage sprouting ornaments and depictions of Jātaka stories, Bharhut. Credit: Indian Museum, Kolkata

Fig. 12 : Female and tree; depiction of a Jātaka story, Bharhut. Credit: Indian Museum, Kolkata

Fig. 13 : Trees and foliage sprouting ornaments and depictions of Jātaka stories, Bharhut. Credit: Indian Museum, Kolkata

Fig. 14 : Trees and foliage sprouting ornaments and depictions of Jātaka stories, Bharhut. Credit: Indian Museum, Kolkata

Fig. 15 : Trees and foliage sprouting ornaments and depictions of Jātaka stories, Bharhut. Credit: Indian Museum, Kolkata

Fig. 16 : Trees and foliage sprouting ornaments and depictions of Jātaka stories, Bharhut. Credit: Indian Museum, Kolkata

Fig. 17 : Trees and foliage sprouting ornaments and depictions of Jātaka stories, Bharhut. Credit: Indian Museum, Kolkata

Fig. 18 : Trees and foliage sprouting ornaments and depictions of Jātaka stories, Bharhut. Credit: Indian Museum, Kolkata

Fig. 19 : Trees and foliage sprouting ornaments and depictions of Jātaka stories, Bharhut. Credit: Indian Museum, Kolkata

Fig. 20 : Trees and foliage sprouting ornaments and depictions of Jātaka stories, Bharhut. Credit: Indian Museum, Kolkata

Fig. 21 :Tree bestowing food and drink; depiction of a Jātaka story, Bharhut. Credit: Indian Museum, Kolkata

I shall leave the deciphering of every detail of this work and the performance to the audience. And I would only say that this performance and its text comes from my inner being, my conflicts, my work as an art historian and as a performer.

The theme of the performance almost demanded that it be performed around a real tree. A tree which would be big enough to cover my body, so that I could hide behind it, make it my entry and exit point, and eventually become one with it. The performance prompted a search for such trees in urban spaces, where I wished to rehearse and perform. Naturally, for the tree to hide me completely, it had to be old and big. And the search for such trees in Delhi and Ljubljana evoked questions and realisations about how landscapes had changed to make way for cities. All the people in Slovenia who hosted this performance had to first hunt for such a tree for the performance to be held. This process itself led to historical details and memories of patterns of deforestation. For instance, in Nova Gorica, in Slovenia, in certain regions it was quite hard to find old trees. I was told that this region was heavily deforested during the World Wars and the forests never managed to recover. My dear friend Tatjana wished to host a performance in the mountains in Laz, Planino Blato but said that the forests are slowly disappearing and moving away. Thus, stories of forests emerged from the story that was told in the performance.

I also wished to convey the mesmerising beauty of forests, trees, rivers and flowers that is so deeply engrained in ancient Indian poetry; the beauty of nature that was far more abundant and resplendent in ancient times. For this I chose perhaps the most enigmatic ancient Indian text, a text which has poetry in small verses and some of which can arguably be assigned to feminine authorship, an extremely rare occurrence. This text is called Gāthāsaptasati, written in Maharashtri Prākṛt and some of its verses can be dated to 200 BCE or before. The poetry in this text talks about the most mundane events of everyday life and in these elements of nature are inseparably entangled. As if it is impossible for life to exist without forests and trees, rivers and flowers. Nature is the life sap of these gāthās. And for me this text and its poetry is the essence of the motif of female and tree.

Urban life has somewhere forgotten these connections and seeks artificial luxury. A few chosen pieces of poetry from this text were kept for the audience to read while waiting for the performance to begin and to take away, as a reminder of those deep connections of mundane life with nature, earthly yet ethereal.

In a way we all are nature spirits, tress spirits and I found many were most welcoming and willing to host this performance that year. These are the details of the people who blessed me with their love –

- Open rehearsal in the park nearby Park hotel, Slovenski Etnografski Muzej, 27 July 2021
- Open rehearsal in the park nearby Park hotel, Slovenski Etnografski Muzej, 10 August 2021
- Performance in village Čepovan, Nadja Velusček's home; hosts: Nadja Velušček and Magda Reja, 1 August 2021
- Performance in the park nearby Park hotel, Slovenski Etnografski Muzej, 15 August 2021
- Performance in the park nearby Park hotel, Slovenski Etnografski Muzej, 17 August 2021
- Performance in the park nearby Park hotel, Slovenski Etnografski Muzej, 19 August 2021
- Performance recording at the Tivoli Park. Filming and editing: Nadja Valentinčič Furlan, Slovenski Etnografski Muzej, 20 August 2021
- Performance in Golo Brdo, Iva and Ivan Skubin gallery garden; hosts: Iva and Ivan Skubin, Magda Reja, 6 September 2021
- Performance at Križ near Sežana, Tončinovadomačija – Majda Škrlj, hosts: Mojca Račič and Majda Škrlj, 25 September 2021
- Performance at Javnizavod Krajinski park Kolpa, nearby Šokčevdvor, hosts: Mojca Račič and Kolpa Krajinski Park, 3 October 2021
- Performance at the center of Ljubljana, Igriška Ulica, host: Tatjana Marušič, 9 October 2021

Fig. 22 : During a rehearsal, Ljubljana, Slovenia. Credit: Tina Palaić

Fig. 23 : Performance at Križ near Sežana, Tončinova domačija – Majda Škrlj, Slovenia. Hosted by Mojca Račič and Majda Škrlj, 25 September 202. Credit: Mojca Račič

catastrophe shooting down on us in different forms. We are made to believe that we are far too advanced in the sciences and technology to be affected. The propaganda of such a thought is geared towards more trade and commercial activity in the garb of economic progress and many times at the cost of human rights violations and self-harm.

For instance, one must question the need for us humans to travel as much as we do today, with all the means of transportation available to us, at the cost of massive deforestation, cutting down of the last of the oldest surviving trees for road widening projects and penetrating mountains to make tunnels at a devastating rate. This is done many times on the pretext of saving nature, ironically, and many times for religious pilgrimage, among other reasons. A deity on a mountain receives worship by an unprecedented number of people at the cost of the mountain itself and at the cost of the surrounding forestation, which were integral to that deity at one time. Economically, one observes that the moment human beings acquire the minimum wealth needed to make such pilgrimage or travel around the world, with the new infrastructure, we immediately opt for it. Does it give us peace and religious merit? Unfortunately, such utilisation of wealth is the aspiration of the majority. Those who cannot afford it yet and the ones who can, share these aspirations of consuming new infrastructure.

As a parallel in a different continent, snow is artificially manufactured for sports. It would be pertinent to view many sports as pure manifestations of human ego, which is never sufficiently satisfied. Many require a levelled field devoid of vegetation and on these world-champions are pronounced. This is not meant to disrespect sportspersons or their hard work. But the idea of such sports is unfortunately infested with negligence towards anything else except personal gains and ego gratification.

Capitalism is the only system that has worked, shall we say? Trade has existed in ancient times. But were we humans ever able to inflict self-harm, just to gain wealth, as we do today? Technology has aided war and capitalism in a hazardous way, to put it subtly. And when the idea of wealth becomes an end in itself, when capitalism becomes an end in itself, overconsumption becomes a way of life and one is bound to be doomed. Greed supplemented with technology, and both governing modern capitalism must be given a fresh term. It is unbridled capitalism.

There is wisdom in much of ancient societies which survived far longer than the so-called modern ones can hope. There were ancient knowledge systems and technologies, far stronger, ecological and viable which we have either lost or chosen to ignore[2]. This is not a blanket statement for everything that existed in the past and for all societies, but a pointer to several such knowledge traditions which have been getting lost with every new mechanised generation. It is also important to see how human concerns have remained somewhat similar from thousands of years. In the *Jātaka* stories (Cowell 1907) from ancient India, one hears of concerns over cutting trees, forests and sharing water sources. These are shockingly close to our modern world than our technological advancements would have us believe. And yet, have we learnt anything from history?

There is no doubt a shepherd's need to cut trees, perhaps for warmth in winter (to make fire) and for the ground to graze his cattle. But what happens if these forests and trees are not replaced? The underground water levels slowly get depleted, and no more grass or water can be retained anymore. For many communities in history and in our modern world, the day has arrived and passed when no more forest remained which could be cut down to make way for grazing, settlement or construction or mining. And yet, mining is a worldwide phenomenon which continues unabated. So, some people are trying to reach the deepest forest reserves of the planet, the Amazon forests[3], for example. This phenomenon too has occurred too many times in the past, more recently in the way of colonialism. But the scale that technological advancements and capitalism[4] has made it possible today is unsurpassable in human history.

Are human species condemned to perish in their own hands? Are we humans, who claim to be the most intelligent of all species, so short-sighted that we cannot see we are on the path to self-destruction?

The Bard, the Storyteller and the Dancer

Why should we tell stories? Because our survival depends on them in more ways than we can imagine. In Indian history, the bard has almost always been the keeper of history (Thapar 1978, 259-285). She or he became the priest sometimes and sometimes remained simply a bard. There is so much that has passed unnoticed and we know only a part of it because someone decided to tell its story. What was told remained, and the rest faded away. It was the bard who chose and preserved history. One can imagine that it gave this record keeper a certain sense of power. It is this power that made the bard a priest. It is hard to imagine the stories and the histories and wisdom lost to us with the decline and subjugation of certain ancient traditions which produced their own folklore. Their bards were either annihilated or converted. Some Indian folklore traditions that have partially survived are *phad* painting and *mātānipachedi* (Singh 1998).

It is in a way, in our very nature to tell stories as much as it is our responsibility, and especially to tell ancient stories, the stories we heard as children, perhaps from elders, our grandparents.

Yakṣī and Stories around her

I have chosen to tell the stories of trees, tree deities, forests and women who lost their own voice in the larger discourses in Indian literature. There were many different cultic traditions in India in the past. However, textual sources from only three, namely Brāhmanical, Buddhist and Jain religions have survived. There is no doubt a diversity of texts within each of these. Some represent local traditions and cultures which these religions tried to assimilate. Tāntrism (Banerji 1988) greatly influenced each of these and so great was the impact that an entirely new stream of rituals and practices evolved, especially in Buddhism as a repercussion (Bhattacharyya 1924; 1932). And yet, when these subjugated and or assimilated some cults, they were inevitably forced to make alterations. They can certainly not be expected to portray the original tenets of the cult they assimilate. And that is why, when we come across references of cults like nature worship (Fergusson 1869; Agrawala 1943; 1965a; 1965b; 1970; 1971), tree deities (DeCaroli 2004), snake cults (Vogel 1926) (*nāga*), or philosophical schools like Lokāyata (Chattopadhyaya 1959; Gokhale 2015), we must remember that these references are being made by the opponents (religions which assimilated or vanquished these cults). And one must be cautious while taking their word literally when searching for the ethos of a cult like tree spirits or nature worship (Barua 1937, 3.72).

No text from the philosophical school of Lokāyata survives today. Other philosophical schools in their books made references to it and many times demonised it. Similarly, there are several references to *nāga* cult[5] and nature deities[6], but all these come from the mouth of those to whom they posed as opponents. We do not really hear the tree worshipping cult in its own voice ever. They must have had their own folklore, with their understanding of the world. But how much of that has reached us today?

My performance is an attempt at understanding the cult of nature worship through a careful and critical reading of ancient Indian texts and folklore. I am fully aware that I can never completely know the past as it existed and my own ideas of the world and times that I am born in will always affect my understanding of these ancient cults. I have my own biases which I cannot do away with and I humbly admit this and clear my standpoint instead of claiming neutrality. Neutrality is simply a myth, something that no one can possibly achieve. Climate change and deforestation are the most pressing concerns of my world, and it is true that I am probably imposing certain ideas of my times upon ancient ones. But who can claim to avoid such a bias? If at all anyone does make such a claim, it is bound to fall apart soon enough. It can also not be denied that historical references do speak about cutting down of trees and deforestation as sometimes a matter of concern. There are references as well to battles and fights over natural resources like river water and land[7].

And yet, it is important that stories are told, reinterpreted in every age and told again. I have tried to look for traces of tree and nature-worshipping cults in ancient Indian literature, whatever remains of it today and have tried to interpret it in my way. I have made new connections, mixed different stories, added dialogues now and then and have thus created a new text, a new story. The

so effectively cleared that not a trace of those forests is left to us today. The region I was born and brought up in is known as trans-Yamuna, east of Delhi[12], that is the 'other' side of the river Yamuna. Today it is one of the most densely populated and polluted regions of the world[13]. The holy river Yamuna like many other rivers of India (Sah 1993) is now a dump yard, full of plastic and chemicals. This region, East Delhi, once had a rocky terrain with forestation. Today the rocks have been so effectively cut down to make place for roads and housing that most of those living here today hardly have any memory of it and my generation is not aware of this recent history at all. Not more than 200 years ago, east Delhi was a virgin region, arguably never inhabited before. Perhaps, this story shall be told another day.

The way the Yamuna River has changed is beyond the imagination of those living in Delhi presently (Forrest 1824; Alday 2018). Red Fort was built on the banks of Yamuna. Today it is only surrounded by roads overloaded with traffic and pollution. For the Delhi metro, though an excellent initiative, when a station was built near the Red Fort, it was made underground compromising the veining strength of this monument of national significance, the inheritance of all humanity, not just of a single nation[14]. Several monuments have suffered a similar fate in different ways[15].

Documentary films have emerged as a strong genre in modern India. Many films have played a strong role in documenting and understanding complex and extremely problematic realities which would have otherwise remained hidden. For instance, documentary filmmaker Priya Thuvassery, in her film titled "Coral Woman"[16] (2019) portrays the sad condition of corals in south of India. Sanjay Kak's films, "Words on water" (2002) and "Red Ant Dream" (2013) bring out issues of how we deal with our natural resources like waterbodies and forests. The docu-fiction film 'Tortoise under the Earth' (2022) by Shishir Jha captures a Uranium mining area in the state of Jharkhand, India and the Sarna[17] community which is forced into losing their land. These are just a few instances in which some long impending and most of the times silenced questions have been raised. This has been possible because of the potential of documentary filmmaking and no doubt some very courageous filmmakers.

While there are a few examples as stated, in most cases we have not documented, discussed and debated what we have, most of the times, changed for the worse. How many examples can one quote from our times[18]? There are just too many.

Shall I speak of tourism plans for the Lakshadweep islands[19]? Where there is absolutely no involvement of the local people, they have no voice, no say in the matter.

Will we be able to save the Aravalli? #Aravalli Bachao or Aarey forests? #saveaarey.

Dehradun, in the foothills of the Himalayas, has a different story to tell[20].

Storytelling as Part of Rituals

Many rituals are primarily based on telling the stories of gods and legends in many religions. In Jainism, Kalpasūtra[21] is narrated. On the occasion of *Karwā Cauth*, mostly practised in north India, stories form the core of rituals (Diamond Books, 2006). In my family, women are expected to listen to this story from their mother-in-law.

The occasion of *Hoi*, a fast a mother is expected to keep for the wellbeing of her children, revolves around stories. The folklore that was told to my mother from my grandmother when she was alive goes as follows. There was once a mother who worshipped plants. Her son, who was a woodcutter becoming extremely unhappy with her rituals and religious practises, decided to leave home and look for work elsewhere. On his travels, he went to a new kingdom, in which he saw an elderly lady extremely upset and lamenting. On asking he discovered, there was to be a public ritual very soon in the kingdom in which every year a man was sacrificed. This man was expected to sit at the core of a holy fire which was built around him. And this year the king had ordered her son to be the man to be sacrificed. On hearing this, the woodcutter tells her not to worry since he is willing to volunteer to be sacrificed in place of her son.

Before he had left home, his mother had given him some seeds and had told him to plant these in the face of danger around him. So, when the time arrived and he was in the middle of the pile of wood which was soon to be lit up, he immediately put the seeds from his mother to soil and they magically grew into big plants around him. When the fire was lit, its heat could not touch him due to the plants around him and he kept repeating the mantra his mother had taught him. The king's soldiers who were observing the fire were surprised when they heard a strange sound from inside the fire and being scared, immediately reported it to the king. The king ordered the fire to be extinguished and finding the man inside alive and well was shocked. On learning that his mother's magical seeds had saved him the king declared that from now on every year this day shall be dedicated to Goddess Hoi, the mother and celebrated by telling this story.

The story had a motif which is also repeated in Mahābhārata, that of Bhim, offering himself as sacrifice in place of the son of the lady, in whose home the Pāṇḍava brothers and their mother lived during their stay in hiding.

It is interesting to see that many stories related to festivals which are extremely regional in nature, essentially non-Brāhmanised until now, have strong female characters. They do not feature any of the prominent Brāhmanical deities, Viṣṇu, Brahmā, Śiva.

Another similar story can be narrated which is told on the occasion of *Karwā Cauth*. A devoted wife had a husband with seven brothers. Each of the brothers also had a wife. On the occasion of *Karwā Cauth*, the brothers' wives, being jealous of her, showed her a fake moon and made her eat before the auspicious hour. Every bite she took was accompanied by a bad omen and the third bite brought the news of her husband's death. Determined to bring her husband back she sat with his corpse until the goddess came to take him away. When the goddess arrived, she held her garment and would not let her go until her husband was restored to her. The goddess told her that her wish can only be granted by the next goddess who shall cross the same path. Six female deities crossed the path and told her to wait for the next one in the same way. The seventh one was the fiercest of all. She appeared with red eyes, eating flesh and with big nails and it was this goddess who finally restored the man to life.

The story clearly refers to the cult of seven mother goddesses and relates it to *Karwā Cauth* which is an attempt at Brāhmanising the cult. Both the rituals mentioned here are centred around storytelling and women. All other rituals are centred around the telling of folklore. After the story, earthen pots filled with water are worshipped with rice, sandal paste, flowers and incense. This water then becomes auspicious. On *Karwā Cauth* the moon is worshipped and on Hoi, stars are considered holy.

The power of these stories lies in their reiteration. The first one, in particular, has a regional earthy flavour. If it was not for the rituals these stories would have probably been forgotten. And thus, stories are reiterated from generations. And these are storehouses of history and value systems and assert identities and belief systems. They are part of the collective memory of a community from hundreds of years ago. History and identity are the foundations for the existence of any community and not merely areas of academic interest. Without a cultural identity, the most essential marker of one's existence, one has nothing to claim for oneself. Protecting and creating identities is dependent on culture and what is termed today as art. The modern idea of nations and nationalism is a derivation of this principle. When an army is created to protect a nation, it is protecting a cultural entity formed of stories[22]. Without this identity, the army will have nothing to defend. In the garb of such a defence many times fake identities and histories are created. Since invariably, war is simply business for some at the cost of the majority.

We are often fed with the idea that an army is more essential than a culture which is a narrative created by the capitalistic modern world centred around business. If there is no culture, no community, no nation can make any claim to nationhood. This culture is dependent on how we treat our stories and what we do with them. This is a pertinent reason why ancient communities found it necessary to bind folklore with rituals which are not given up easily.

Kathak: the Form of Storytellers

The earliest documentation available on the dance form Kathak links it to a community of storytellers (Trivedi 2012; Bose 1999), are in a position of power and make choices that suit their agenda, especially in terms of aesthetics. The art must, according to their choices, subscribe to Euro-American aesthetics. This is one example of how colonialism operates in present times.

In the colonised regions of the world, coloniality (Vázquez 2009) functions at a different level. Beginning with language, English and the knowledge of it is seen as 'modern' or 'highly educated' or 'high class'. This penetrates academics in India quite successfully. More than what you write, how you write it in English is considered more important. If your English is not 'perfect', irrespective of your research, most international journals will not accept your work. Within India, many places (and many scholars) consider the writings of European-American scholars more important and worthy of being quoted in research and writing than the best of Indian scholarship. If a drastically different methodology is introduced by an Indian scholar, it is not taken note of, but the same approach by a European scholar is highly applauded. Europeans and Americans, especially scholars, are welcomed in museums and galleries; Indians do not receive the same treatment. The curriculum followed in most art, design and fashion colleges in India focus mostly on Euro-centric history, costume, art and aesthetics; Indian history of costume, design, Indian aesthetics, Indian methods of artmaking and so much more is completely sidelined.

In modern urban architecture in India, architects have given-up Indian elements which are better suited to the country's land and climate and more ecological. The Indian kitchen (in which one must sit on the floor and cook as well as eat) can hardly be traced in urban Indian houses. It is replaced by modular standing kitchens which are not best suited to Indian cooking which requires, sometimes, more time and patience. Especially in modern Indian architecture, an entire Indian way of life and outlook is compromised.

Technology and Motivations Behind It

One must ask, what has modern technology (which is primarily a repercussion of the discovery of electricity, and it is being utilised for mechanical reproduction) given us? It has been a primary tool in the hands of the colonisers. Capitalism has convinced us that the human species are at its peak with this technology. We are taught to measure everything, including happiness, with Gross Domestic Product (GDP) (not as Gross Domestic Happiness, an alternative suggested by Bhutan). It was a known fact that most technological inventions and 'advancements' were initially done for the purpose of warfare, that is, destruction and mass killing in the name of patriotism, in reality, dictated by capitalist interests, for harnessing profits for a handful of people. Eventually these technologies trickled down into the lives of the masses.

There are a few things that have benefited human civilization. Some of these have come not as technology but at an ideological level. One of these is the idea of human rights. At a technological level, the discovery of bio-enzymes is significant as a replacement to so many chemical-based cleaning agents (creations of industry-based capitalism) which devastate an ecosystem. The invention of Crypto-currency (a blockchain-based technology) is path-breaking since it works with DeFi (Decentralised Finance) and will hopefully challenge the corrupt, almost failed banking systems across the world and be an alternative to the failing economies of so many countries. This is not to deny that a lot of black money is being converted into crypto currency (many including economist Paul Krugman are completely against crypto currency) and the manufacture of it requires immense consumption of energy. Though wrong use of energy and non-renewable sources is far more massive outside of the crypto world, even though alternatives like hydrogen power are already in use. However, the crypto currency world is extremely inaccessible due to its technological nature and frauds and manipulations possible within the vulnerable points on the ecosystem. For instance, it is possible for a developer to obfuscate a transaction on Ethereum blockchain and literally 'steal' on the slippage in crypto currency coins while a transaction is still pending. Such practices are obviously done with the intension of making 'profit' or money and it is possible to employ bots to do so at a large scale. In such cases, no doubt, capitalism again is dictating the terms[30].

Crypto currency has changed the way we perceive our world. However, the future will tell the story of this technological intervention.

For the accumulation of knowledge, technology has been employed for archaeology and massive excavations across the world. The history of colonial excavations (Moro-Abadia 2006) and transfer of artifacts (Barrett 1954), wealth (Dutt 1893; Habib 1975, 2006, 2013) and human remains to the homeland of colonisers has been told by many. There is a recent development in the conversations around repatriation, especially human remains to their rightful descendants from colonised states (Rassool 2015; Silvester 2019).

There has now risen an ethical debate (Clegg 2020) around exhibiting human remains in public. What has been ignored is that in many cases archaeological excavations have led to vandalism of the site as well as the remains[31]. Whenever an archaeological site is excavated and the documentation of the findings are not published in the form of an official archaeological report, the site and the artifacts recovered face an immediate threat of loss of documentation and thus, significant information connected to the site is lost[32]. The exact finding spot of any object, the level in the ground at which it was discovered, the state in which it was found, and so much more, if not immediately documented and preserved, will surely be lost in procrastination or negligence.

Excavations continue to take place, in which human remains are lifted from their resting places and taken to a completely different location, far away from their context to a place where they were never meant to be, a place where the ancestors, our ancestors who buried them and those who were buried never wished to be. All this is done in the name of knowledge and preservation. One must ask if we are truly able to preserve these. Excavations and removal of human remains must be undertaken only if there is reason to believe that they are under some immediate threat. There are and were so many artifacts under threat from terrorist groups and the world with all its dialogue around knowledge and preservation, did nothing to save these (for instance Bamiyan Buddha(Warikoo 2002, Rowland 1974)). So why are excavations conducted with so much enthusiasm and celebrated in the media? Is it truly about preservation or mere ego satisfaction? Do not the ancestors from thousands of years ago deserve far more respect and dignity than recent ones[33]?

Thus, in most cases, since its inception, electricity-based technology has been misused to subjugate and in some cases for genocide (not just in the case of Nazism, but also the term must be used for the mass killing of forest-dwelling communities across the world and the annihilation of their culture and the forests they have lived in for millennia).

Coming back to ancestors, stories, in the form of folklore, have preserved and revered their memory far more successfully than modern technology-based archaeology might be able to do. Will our virtual database last for more than two thousand years? Folklore from some cultures, including India, have lasted longer. Can we guarantee that we will be able to preserve for more than three thousand years what we so heroically excavate and then glorify ourselves for it?

Fig. 24 : During performance shoot at Tivoli Park, Ljubljana, Slovenia. Credit: Nadja Valentinčič Furlan

The Cursed Land of Lustful Women : The Performance

She comes out of the tree admiring the beauty of it and its flowers. Picking those flowers, she makes a garland and adorns herself. She picks fruits and begins preparing wine and sitting under the tree, she begins to remember…

Once upon a time, when Brahmadatta was the king of Vārāṇasī…

Jātaka tales, the stories of Buddha's past lives, almost always consist of this phrase. The stories begin with an incident within the lifetime of Buddha, which prompts the Buddha to tell a story from one of his past lives. The Buddha relates the incident to his past life and also identifies others from the story to their present birth. The beginning of these past lives is almost always stated as this phrase

> "Once upon a time, when Brahmadatta was the king of Vārāṇasī…."

The structure is that of storytelling and this is done, in the *Jātakas*, in order to convey a moral value or the Buddhist teaching.

My first story begins with an instance in Kumbha *Jātaka* (No. 512) in which Buddha responds to a query of his follower Viśākhā concerning the origins of strong drinks. Buddha condemns drinking and says that it brings deterioration of character in both men and women. Viśākhā, a devout follower of Buddha and known as one of his greatest patrons, is accompanied by many of her female friends to listen to the sermons of Buddha on the occasion of a drinking festival proclaimed at Sāvatthi. Disgusted by these 'drunken' female friends of Viśākhā, especially by their dancing 'improper' gestures and laughter, Buddha tells the story of the origin of drink (wine).

This story which tells us how the first ever wine or strong drink came to be in the world is most curious in nature. Unlike Brāhmanical stories, which attribute the origin of almost everything to one of their gods or some incident in their life, this Buddhist tale says that nature, in the form of a tree, was the cause of the first ever strong drink to be.

And the performance says—

> "Once upon a time, when Brahmadatta was the king of Vārāṇasī. There was a certain tree that sprang up to the height of a man with his arms extended. In the midst of its three forks, was a hole, as big as a wine jar and when it rained this hole, was filled up with water.
>
> Round about the tree grew some fruit plants and a pepper shrub; and the ripe fruits from these when they were cut down, fell into the hole.

Not far from the tree was some self-grown paddy. Parrots would pluck the heads of rice and eat them and perched on this tree. And while they were eating this paddy and the husked rice fell into the hole.

Fermenting through the sun's heat, this water assumed a blood red colour.

In the hot season, flocks of birds being thirsty, drank of it and becoming intoxicated, fell at the foot of the tree, and after sleeping a while, flew away, chirping merrily. And the same thing happened in the case of wild dogs, monkeys and other creatures."

The story in the *Jātaka* continues from here on, with a man, a forester noticing this drink and trying it and then along with an ascetic friend selling it to different kings.

My story in a way concludes here with these lines…

"They say it was a woman who discovered the secret of making wine. She used to worship trees. Or perhaps, she was, the tree goddess, herself."

Attributing the discovery of drink to a woman makes more sense to me, in the light of the fact that forest communities existed which were, at least some of them, matriarchal. They had a female as the head of the clan. This is the case with Tāṅakā, in Rāmāyaṇa, who is called a *yakṣī* and is the head of a forest clan. Tāṅakā used to attack Brahmins when they wanted to conduct yajna, or their ritual sacrifices in the forest. She has been demonised in the Brāhmanical Rāmāyaṇa. Her side of the story has never been told. The forest being the land of her people was under immediate threat if any Brahmin performed a *yajña* in it, since it was symbolic of their taking it over. As the head of her clan, it was her duty to protect the forest and her people and she was killed in the attempt, according to the story of Rāmāyaṇa. This is of course, the Brāhmanical version of the story. The Buddhist story, which is also evidently patriarchal, claims that a man discovered the secret of making wine.

In my story the female who discovers this secret, is herself a secret, an enigma. The performer, that is me, changes in an instant into the tree deity, the goddess herself.

With this interchanging of roles and a sense of mystery, it is established that the female in this performance, in both the seemingly unconnected stories, is probably the tree deity herself.

The pose of the performer here is that of the so-called 'Dancing Girl' of Harappa.

Fig. 25 : The pose of the Harappan Dancing girl. During performance shoot at Tivoli Park, Ljubljana, Slovenia. Credit: Nadja Valentinčič Furlan

This story is followed by a sort of 'parallel' narrative made through dance without any dialogues. To roughly describe this part in a few words -

> *She is reminded of the wine she was making and turns back to it. Seeing that it is prepared, she remembers her lover and thinks of calling him, but how? She decides to write him a letter on a leaf* (see fig. 26) *and gives it to the wind to take it to him. She then, caresses the tree and waits for him impatiently, turning back to see if he is there (taking of pose of Ravi Varma's Śakuntalā, in which Śakuntalā, the nāyikā/heroine of Kālidās's play Abhijñānaśākuntalam*[34] (see fig. 27, 28) *(Karmarkar 1952), turns back on the pretence of picking a thorn off her foot, to see her lover*[35]*).*
>
> *Alas, he arrives. Embracing him, she offers the wine to the tree, to her lover and drinks herself.*

Fig. 26 : Patralekhana (girl writing a love letter), a common theme in Indian art. During performance shoot at Tivoli Park, Ljubljana, Slovenia. Credit: Nadja Valentinčič Furlan

Fig. 27 : Like Ravi Varma's Śakuntalā, feigning to remove a thorn from her foot, searching/eagerly waiting for her lover. During performance shoot at Tivoli Park, Ljubljana, Slovenia. Credit: Nadja Valentinčič Furlan

Fig. 28 : Śakuntalā by Ravi Varma; feigning to remove a thorn from her foot, to take another look at her lover.
Credit: Sri Chitra Art Gallery, Thiruvananthapuram, Kerala.

Here begins the second part -

"Once upon a time, when Brahmadatta was the king of Vārāṇasī. Having a huge army, he seized upon the kingdom of Kosala, slayed its king and captured the chief queen. He made her his chief consort. At that time the queen was pregnant. And eventually she gave birth to a little girl. She was called princess Kaṇhā. And the king being childless was greatly pleased and bestowed a boom upon the little girl."

(*Princess* Kaṇhā *is seen playing around the tree and worshipping it.*)

"Princess Kaṇhā grew up to be a beautiful lady. One day her father announced an assembly of men so that princess Kaṇhā could choose a deserving husband.

The palace yard was full of men, in all their splendour. And princess Kaṇhā, with her basket full of flowers stood looking out of the window but approved of none of them, until her eyes fell upon those five sons of king Pāṅḍu."

(*Princess* Kaṇhā *is seen doing sṛṅgāra, decorating herself and then begins to worship the tree.*)

Fig. 29 : Female holding a mirror to herself, Bharhut. Credit: Indian Museum, Kolkata

"They say the five sons of king Pāṅḍu burnt an entire forest, to build their city. The five sons of king Pāṅḍu burnt all the trees and killed everyone in the forest to build their city, their palace of illusions, the palace princess Kaṇhā was to be the queen of. She was to be the queen of..."

(Princess Kaṇhā *removes her ornaments, opens her hair in anger, caresses her tree, and walks forward.)*

"What shall I do with these discourses of yours? I have gone over like the first of Goddess Uṣā. Go back to your destiny. I am as hard to get as the wind."

(She walks forward, picks the oil lamp in both hands, walks to the tree, keeps it in front of it, goes to the tree, caresses it. She touches her open hair, throws them back, staring at the audience and disappears behind the tree.)

The character princess Kaṇhā comes from various historical sources. This story has been partly taken from Kuṇāla*Jātaka* (number 536) in which princess Kaṇhā is married to the five brothers, sons of king Pāṅḍu and falls in love with a hump-backed dwarf, with whom she is sexually involved. The *Jātaka* is told to convey to other men the lustful character of all womanhood, which according to the story is beyond correction or 'repair'. The following verse is from Cowell's translation of Kaṇḍina *Jātaka* (number 13) which has not been used in the performance, but which quite evidently portrays the misogyny embedded in this and many other ancient stories -

Cursed be the dart of love that works men pain!
Cursed be the land where women rule supreme!
And cursed the fool that bows to woman's sway!

The title of this performance is derived from various such verses which repeatedly make similar accusations against all womenfolk. I shall not discuss the possible historical repercussions of this narrative here. I have tried to dwell upon it in my Ph.D. thesis in detail (Gupta 2022).

The story of princess Kaṇhā also appears in the epic Mahābhārata. Kaṇhā has been mentioned as the *sakhi*, friend of Krishna, the greatest of heroes, the divine force in the story of Mahābhārata. In this epic, Kaṇhā, also named Draupadi, is married to the five sons of king Pāṅḍu and is deeply humiliated in the royal assembly house of her in-law's family, the Kurus. The husbands of Draupadi, lose her over a game of dice. She is then violently forced into the assembly hall by her brother-in-law, Dushyant, the cousin of the Pāṅḍu brothers, who pulls her by her open hair and then attempts to undress her in front of everyone. According to the story she is 'saved' from disgrace by the magical powers of Krishna. However, she vows revenge and swears that she shall leave her hair untied until one of her husbands brings her Dushyant's blood by tearing open his chest, to wash away the insult.

When I touch my open hair, towards the end of the performance, it is a reference to this vengeance that Kaṇhā seeks, of course in a very different way and against her own to-be or not-to-be-husbands in my performance.

It is also mentioned in Mahābhārata that the Pāṅḍavas, the five brothers, were given Khāṇḍavaprastha during the division of land between the cousins. This Khāṇḍavaprastha was a deep dense forest inhabited by many communities (forest dwellers). The forest was so thick that the only way to clear and thus conquer it was with the help of Agni, that is, fire. The Pāṅḍava brothers, therefore, burnt the forest and many died in this fire. Among the forest communities, lived Maya (also called Mayāsura), known to be a great architect. He was spared by the Pāṅḍavas on the condition that he shall build a mesmerising palace for them. The palace that Maya built was called the 'The palace of illusion' since it was full of splendours and had many visual illusions. Duryodhan, on his visit to this palace, during Rājasūya *yajña,* falls for one such illusion and is insulted by Draupadi.

Historians have remarked upon this incident of the burning of forests as a landmark event that hastened the processes of changing landscape and what is termed as 'climate change' today. Romila Thapar has pointed out that the Gangetic plains were unimaginably thickly forested, once upon a time. These forests have been cleared so effectively, that it is hard to imagine the landscape as it once was.

Nandita Krishna has also observed that "the great changes to the environment through expanding agriculture, intensive farming, deforestation, the decimation of wildlife and so on had a major impact on the people and on historical events". In her words, 'decimation and gradual desertification of land' has always impacted human societies and led to their impoverishment. 'The dependence of human beings towards nature and their duties towards plants and sentient beings', she says, 'has been documented in historical literary sources, archaeology and inscriptions'.

Commenting upon the nature of myths she says -

> "Much of ancient memory has been designated as myths by western scholars. But let's not forget that mythology has been described as the science of primitive man, his manner of explaining the universe." (Krishna 2020)[36]

And further discussing historical ecological changes and concerns, her remarks are significant -

"Only humans have the ability and have spread in every ecosystem. Through technology, they have dominated ecosystems and extracted food, shelter, clothing, energy and material goods. Only humans also have the capacity and the ability to endanger and destroy ecosystems. When human societies have extracted more than the ecosystem can give the environment collapses and can no longer sustain life. Over a period of time, excess populations formed new groups and exploited new areas. Requirement of land and food resulted in intensive agriculture, clash of civilisations, wars between societies and the domination of technically advanced societies over the less advanced, who were used as slaves. In semi-agrarian communities the ownership of food passed from communal sharing to individuals to the state and to institutions, such as temples and so on, who collected, stored and distributed or sold the food. This was to result in the emergence of stratified society with a ruling, military and religious hierarchy, a large population of farmers and craftspeople and the slaves who were the conquered hunter-gatherers."

This is a rare instance of an Indian historian taking note of changes in landscape and its ecological impact due to human activity.

It is also noteworthy that Krishna notes the ecological consequences of different modes of living in human societies. For instance, she says that 'the environmental impact of food gathering, including shifting cultivation was very low', since she says, 'people hunted or collected only what they needed'.

Dilip Menon has taken note of the human centric approach pre-eminent in most of the histories that have yet been recorded and that it is essential that we now consider 'a larger canvas' which consists of nature and wildlife. He touches upon the subject of what has hitherto remained ignored within the paradigm of history (Menon 2021)[37].

He also mentions two major so-called 'revolutions' in the history of human species (38:00 in the mentioned lecture in the endnotes), that is the agricultural revolution and the industrial revolution. Within the context of climate change, these have had an extreme impact on human lives and patterns of migration.

Romila Thapar (1995) also discusses the alienation of the forest and those living in it in ancient India. She considers the dichotomous nature of the village and the forest and how this separation becomes increasingly visible in Rāmāyaṇa and Mahābhārata. She refers to the incidents from Mahābhārata like the hunt that Duṣyanta goes for, in the forest and thus encounters Śakuntalā and the Pāṅḍavas using fire to clear the forest in order to build their capital. Throughout these references, the people living in the forests are treated as uncivilised and as those who are eventually conquered and thus, enslaved. She has also taken note of the persecution of forests that we are silent witnesses of in our times (Thapar 2007, 41).

Dhavalikar (1999; 2002) has proposed a theory on patterns of urbanization dependent on climatic changes across the world. These changes which occurred almost at the same time across the world affected growth and decline of urban cities. According to this theory climatic conditions shift between periods of aridity and humidity. However, these changes seem to occur without any apparent cause. According to him, urbanization could occur only when the climate was favourable and not in periods of aridity despite the familiarity with iron. Dhavalikar suggests that urbanization was more dependent on this kind of climate change rather than use of iron alone. He does not talk about climate change in the past or present as a repercussion of human action and does not view it as a crisis. Ray (2016) discusses various theories around patterns of urbanization and their cause in which he describes Dhavalikar's views along with others.

The last dialogue of the performance is as follows -

"What shall I do with these discourses of yours? I have gone over like the first of Goddess Uṣā. Go back to your destiny. I am as hard to get as the wind."

This is a verse from Rig Veda book 10 Hymn 95. To be precise this line is 10.95.2, which is the second line or verse from the long dialogue that is stated in the Rig Veda as hymn 95.

This is a dialogue between two characters, namely Urvaśī and Pururava. These are rather famous names in the world of ancient Indian stories since Pāṅḍavas trace descent from the glorious king Pururava who apparently falls in love with a celestial nymph called Urvaśī. Their story has been referred to in many later ancient Indian texts, which can be dated post Rig Veda. The Gupta period Indian poet Kālidāsa (Mirashi 1969) wrote a play taking inspiration from this theme which was called *Vikramorvaśiyam*.

All the textual references to this story differ in some way and in some ways they are similar which becomes a point of interest for historian D.D. Kosambi, whose interpretations of Indian myths and history still remain unparalleled. In his pioneering work (Kosambi 1962, 42-81) Myth and Reality, he has written an essay titled 'Urvaśī and Pururavas' which deals primarily with the myth of these two characters.

Considering that there are many versions and interpretations of the myth involving these two characters (all of which are discussed by Kosambi), the narrative can only be roughly sketched here. It goes thus—

Puruvara falls in love with Urvaśī who belongs to a different world, which is heaven. There are hurdles in their union, but they are finally married. Obviously, there are further obstructions in their relationship, but Urvaśī eventually bears him a child. This event itself is a marker of the end of their bond (in some versions) since after bearing a child upon him Urvaśī must return to heaven. What becomes of Puruvara remains rather uncertain in many versions.

Kosambi, after making a comparative study of various versions, suggests that Pururava is to be sacrificed after bearing a child upon

Urvaśī. This reference, he says, is a vestige of the ritual of human sacrifice which was practised sometime in the ancient Indian past in matriarchal societies. A promising man, one of the best of the tribe was chosen to unite with the priestess of the community and after bearing a child to her, he was to be sacrificed.

When Urvaśī says that she has gone over like the first of Goddess Uṣā, she refers to another Vedic female deity 'Uṣā' who is the goddess of dawn. The verse in Rig Veda reads -

I have gone over like the first of the Uṣās.

And not—

I have gone over like the first of Goddess Uṣā.

The term goddess was inserted in the text to make it a little more meaningful, at least to make the phrase somewhat sensible to the audience, even if it still does not convey any direct meaning. The plural form,Uṣās, which is actually used in Rig Veda was also changed to singular to the same effect. The exact meaning of this phrase is now lost and is open to interpretation. Kosambi interprets it to say that after Urvaśī gets a child, she attains a 'higher' status, that of Uṣā. My idea in the performance is also not to curb the phrase by giving it only a single direct meaning. But it is being said in a very different context in the performance text, which is after princess Kaṇhā realises the burning of the forests by the Pāṅḍava brothers.

Uṣā in the Rig Veda is also referred to by Kosambi as a female deity which was once very important but eventually lost her position, especially with the rise of the battle god Indra. The instance of the battle between Indra and Uṣā, referred to in the Rig Veda, is interpreted by him as cultic rivalry or war. In this battle Uṣā is defeated, thus representing the taking over of patriarchal order.

So, in a way Uṣā becomes symbolic of a lost battle and yet, she once had the highest status.

Is it the end?

Stories do not really have an end. Every end is a new beginning. And when one wants to hear ancient tales, there are always many versions. Each version gives us a glimpse of a different line of thought. Each one has something special about it.

The stories in this text have a seemingly simple narrative which leads to certain conclusions and yet, there are so many layers that one begins to see eventually. There is much which is unsaid, making the structure far more complex than it appears to be in the first reading.

A typical folk story is expected to be simple in its structure with a straightforward conclusion. But when interpreted in a historical and social context it may convey social complexities and changes which a community attempted to deal with through these stories. Every community tried to explain phenomena beyond comprehension and unfathomable social changes in their own way, through stories. Urban narratives are generally more complex within their structure.

This text has been inspired from *Jātaka* stories which have a distinct folk character and yet the narrative has been changed and built to become far more complex and leaves much to the audience's imagination. There are many suggestions in the text and in the performed narrative which is not spelt out in words. Even within the stories put into words, not everything is revealed. What does she do, in the performance, after she discovers that the Pāṅḍavas had burnt that forest? I have been asked sometimes after the performance. Are the two stories linked in any way? Does she actually marry them? What happens to the five men? In the last verse she says, 'I have gone over', gone over what? And how? I will not attempt to answer all the questions.

Epilogue

Once upon a time, when Brahmadatta was the king of Vārāṇasī…

We shall witness her with a different face, from yet another world. What will she be this time? A queen? An ascetic? A bard?

Perhaps…

Fig. 30 : Performance at Križ near Sežana, Tončinova domačija – Majda Škrlj, Slovenia. Hosted by Mojca Račič and Majda Škrlj, 25 September 2021. Credit: Mojca Račič

Notes

1. There are various methods in which myths can be interpreted. One of these methods, as suggested by Indian Marxist scholarship, particularly D.D. Kosambi (1962), is to trace vestiges of historical changes and realities in them (Gupta 2018).
2. Our Traditional water management systems of India are a great example. They are far more ecological than the modern water dams. A recent conference titled, 'Traditional Water Systems of India: A Heritage for the future', 22-23 September 2022, elaborates upon this extensively. This was organised by Faculty of Architecture, CEPT University, Ahmedabad, Gujarat in hybrid mode. There are endless examples for this. Traditional agricultural practices as opposed to use of chemical fertilizers and pesticides are ecological and provide nutritious food. Handwoven natural fabrics as opposed to use to polyester.
3. Deforestation in Amazon forests is highly underreported, like all other climate change related issues. https://www.bbc.com/news/world-latin-america-59341770 excessed on 29 January 2022.
4. We are all bound, and in certain ways, chained by capitalism. Trade has existed in ancient times across the world, but the scale of it, today, is unprecedented due to technology and its interventions. The way capitalism functions today (at a global level and aided with technology), it has the power to destroy anything and anyone for personal gains. It is, in fact, self-destructive.
5. *Nāga* cult has been subjugated by all the three religions, Brāhmanism, Buddhism and Jainism in their visual imagery as well as their texts. Geetika Kher has done an in-depth study of the subjugation of the *nāga* cult (Kher 2006, 9-52).
6. There are ample references to tree deities in *Jātaka* stories in which they appear as subjugated entities.
7. The battle of Mahābhārata was fought over a piece of land which of course is translated as a matter of dignity and pride. Sutta Nipāta Aṭṭhakathā 2.362 mentions the story of the conflict between the Śākyans and Koliyans over the water of river Rohiṇī for irrigating their agricultural fields. Buddha arrives on the scene as a peacemaker and tells them a story which is also narrated as Daddabha*Jātaka* (no. 322).
8. The word *sūtradhāra* is used within the context of Indian theatre for which the most ancient Indian text intact today is Nāṭyaśāstra attributed to Bharata (Ghosh 1951) as well as Indian sculpture (Sarawati 1975) and architecture. *Sūtradhāra* is the person who holds the threads,

that is, controls everything. In a previous work, I and my co-author have described the function of *sūtradhāra* within the context of Ellora (Kannal, Gupta 2019).

9. Buddha was born under a tree. His mother, queen Māyā was carried under a tree when she was having birth pains. This was done so that she receives the blessings of the tree deity. It was a difficult childbirth and Māyā died within few days after the birth of her child. Buddha also received enlightenment under a tree. Many such stories are found in the writings of Buddhaghosa (Law 1923).
10. There is an ancient text, Gāthāsaptaśatī (Mehrotra 1991, reprint 2008) which consists of love poetry in Mahārāṣṭrīan Prākrit (one of the five kinds of Prākrit used in ancient India). It describes nature in its diverse ways in great profusion. One of the couplets which has been used in this performance talks about the traveller being invited under the shade of a tree.
11. D.D. Kosambi (1962, 82-109) describes the role of crossroads in ancient India in detail in his article "At the Crossroads: A Study of Mother Goddess Cult Sites."
12. https://dmeast.delhi.gov.in/history/ (Accessed on 13 March 2022).
13. A complete record of how the landscape of Delhi and East Delhi in particular has changed over the last hundred years is missing. Recent years have seen more media attention towards the increasing pollution levels of Delhi among other Indian cities. https://www.downtoearth.org.in/blog/air/fighting-air-pollution-in-delhi-for-2-decades-a-short-but-lethal-history-67585 (accessed on 13 March 2022).
14. There is news of another metro project in the city of Agra which might have a similar or worse impact on heritage monuments. https://www.newslaundry.com/2021/03/11/why-agras-metro-rail-may-wreck-its-historical-heritage-and-environment (Accessed on 13 March 2022).
15. Meghal Arya (2019), an Associate Professor at the Faculty of Architecture, CEPT University, Ahmedabad has discussed many cases of heritage monuments under threat in her work.
16. https://www.youtube.com/watch?v=YBpbuwH6nCg (accessed on 14 March 2022).
17. Sarna is a religion from India that believes in tree worship. Sal tree among others is considered a sacred grove.
18. The initiative "Let India breathe" can be mentioned here. https://www.letindiabreathe.in/ (accessed on 14 March 2022).
19. https://www.change.org/p/shri-ram-nath-kovind-the-president-of-the-republic-of-india-halt-unsustainable-tourism-development-in-lakshadweep (accessed on 14 March 2022). This is a petition which

speaks in detail of the tourism plan in Lakshadweep Islands. There is a pdf embedded on this webpage where the complete petition with further references can be accessed.

20. https://www.change.org/p/chief-minister-of-uttarakhand-save-dehradun-s-10000-trees-from-being-chopped-for-an-airport?recruiter=470558182&recruited_by_id=eabbdcc0-bf74-11e5-8f67-53ecf7f4c69b&utm_source=share_petition&utm_medium=copylink&utm_campaign=psf_combo_share_initial&utm_term=psf_combo_share_initial (accessed on 14 March 2022). This is a petition titled "Save Dehradun's 10,000 Trees from being Cut for an Airport Expansion".
21. Many ancient Indian texts including Kalpasūtra have been translated in the volumes titled "Sacred Books of the East". Kalpasūtra has been translated by Herman Jacobi (1879; 1884).
22. For instance, the Sambalpuri poet, Haldhar Nag from Bargarh, Odisha, who has recently been awarded Padma Shri, the fourth highest civilian award of India, writes poetry in Kosli, an endangered language. By writing poetry in this language, he has saved it and protected its identity more than any armed force could ever imagine doing. https://www.thebetterindia.com/50523/padma-shri-haldhar-nag-poet-phd/ (accessed on 14 March 2022).
23. Sahapedia, an online resource on art and culture, has a series of articles on Kathak written by a Kathak practisioner, Siddhi Goel. Within the context of use of syllables in Kathak the following article is useful. https://www.sahapedia.org/looking-the-origins-of-kathak-journey-the-16th-20th-century (accessed on 16 March 2022).
24. The role of the spectator is considered extremely important in Indian aesthetics, which is a distinct character of the Indian tradition. The spectator, though helped by the artist in this endeavour, is expected to be free of biases and pre-occupation while experiencing a work of art. Pre-occupation is considered as a rasavighna (hurdle in the process of aesthetic experience) by the great Indian aesthete Abhinavagupta (Gupta 1987), from Kashmir in 10-11th century CE. He discusses this vighna (hurdle) in his theory saptarasavighna (the seven hurdles to the aesthetic experience and how to overcome them). A useful compilation of Indian aesthetic (Devy 2010) theories can be found in the course books of IGNOU self-learning material. https://www.lkouniv.ac.in/site/writereaddata/siteContent/202004120632194475nishi_Indian_Poetics.pdf (accessed on 16 March 2022). https://egyankosh.ac.in/bitstream/123456789/34686/1/Unit-4.pdf (accessed on 16 March 2022).

25. Lacchu Maharaj (https://www.youtube.com/watch?v=qH_tw1NwswU, accessed on 16 March 2022) and Shambhu Maharaj (https://www.youtube.com/watch?v=QNtbWvocT6g, accessed on 16 March 2022) demonstrate this most beautifully.
26. Sitara devi discusses this in detail in an interview with Kapila Vatsyayan. Vatsyayan (1991, 1996, 1997) was an institution builder who created the archives of Indira Gandhi National Centre for the Arts, Delhi. She has extensively interviewed various performing artists. These interviews and a lot of other previous records are preserved in the archives of IGNCA, Delhi. https://www.youtube.com/watch?v=bgh-jljPiT0 (in Hindi, no subtitles, accessed on 16 March 2022).
27. In an interview T.M. Krishna discusses his dilemmas while talking about his book, 'Reshaping Art', 2018. https://www.youtube.com/watch?v=ue1aQY0ANIo&t=148s (accessed on 16 March 2022).
28. In one of his writings titled 'Riddles in Hinduism', specifically Riddle number 22, 'Brahmā is not Dharma: What good is Brahmā?', B.R. Ambedkar (BAWS 1987) refers to the concepts of Brahmāism, Brāhmanism and Vedānta in detail. The annotated critical selection published by Navayana press (Anand 2016) does complete justice to this piece of Ambedkar's writing in adding so many notes and details which are extremely useful for a better understanding of Ambedkar's work.
29. Being able to create an 'even' or equal society is a myth. It is impossible, an ideal state that cannot exist and can only be imagined. Ideals are like the polar star. They can be seen from a distance, but one can never reach them. Another example is the Kantian idea of universal beauty. This is one of the problems of Marxist theory. People can never be equal because humans are not machines. Hierarchies are bound to exist (T.M. Krishna also delves into this paradox in the interview referred to in this work). But it is also human nature and survival instinct to go against hierarchies and exploitation. One cannot view any group of people or class as necessarily a positive or negative force. Marxism sees one class as exploited and the other as the exploiter which is a problematic proposition.
30. Dan Robinson and Georgios Konstantopoulos describe this as a horror story. The title of their article, interesting, is "Ethereum is a dark forest" which is inspired from a science fiction novel "The Dark Forest" by Liu Cixin, 2008. Its noteworthy that the perception of a forest even in this age of claimed hyper-modernity, luxury and technologically pathbreaking inventions and machinery is that of being dark, unexplored and as a place of immediate threat to one's

existence. There are unforeseen dangers in forests, no doubt. But modern science and fiction continues to see nature in the form of a forest as opposed to and thus, as an enemy and dangerous to human existence. This is in complete contradiction to the way nature is perceived by so many communities who have been living in forests till date. We must remember, all human beings once lived in forests only. This is the article I have referred to - https://www.paradigm.xyz/2020/08/ethereum-is-a-dark-forest/ accessed on 30 January 2022.

31. Naman Ahuja (2019) discusses how laws, particularly in India, are only making the situation for the preservation of artefacts more difficult. He has also pointed out that it is urbanisation that is "the main driving force for the desacralisation *(differently spelled)* of, or pillaging of ancient sites".
32. Two examples of such archaeological sites from India are Burzahom in Kashmir (Kaw 2004, 79) and Dholavira in Gujarat. The archaeological report of Burzahom not yet been published. In case of Dholavira which was excavated for many seasons since 1989-90, a draft of the excavation report (Bisht 2015; 2018) came out only in 2015. Before this some articles were written on this site on specific aspects (Bisht 1993).
33. There is an Egyptian mummy in Indian museum Kolkata which is placed in a small room on public display. The humidity levels of this room are extremely high and not well suited for it. The following are instances of the little media attention it has received- https://www.news18.com/news/lifestyle/travel-egypt-keen-to-help-restore-mummy-at-indian-museum-1369298.html , https://www.thehindu.com/sci-tech/science/mummy-at-indian-museum-moderately-stable-says-expert/article28984844.ece (both accessed on 12th March 2022)
34. https://www.youtube.com/watch?v=e4J9ocVOnh8 (Accessed on 12th March 2022) B.L. Institute of Indology, Delhi organised the lecture अभिज्ञानशाकुन्तले देवनागरी पाठ में नयी गवेषणा। (*Abhijñānaśākuntala ke Devanāgarīpāṭh me nayī gaveṣaṇā*) online on 2nd Jan 2021, by Vasantkumar M. Bhatt, Head of the Department of Sanskrit and Director, School of Languages, Gujarat University, Ahmedabad.
35. Śakuntalā and Kālidāsa became the choice of Hindu nationalists because of the portrayal of this female character as the epitome of delicacy and her dependence on her hero as opposed to Vasantasenā, the heroine of the play *Mṛichchhakaṭika* (Kale 1924) of Śūdraka, who is a strong and independent character (Mukherji 2011, 90-110).

36. https://www.youtube.com/watch?v=h5X8HWQJPEU(1:22:00) Accessed on 31 December 2021. Webinar on " Issues and Perspectives in Indology" 20th November 2020, ICCR Official.
37. https://www.youtube.com/watch?v=7JHzYYKI0MQAccessed on 31 December 2021. Thinking with the Present: Writing Histories of Water, Dilip Menon delivered this lecture on 11 December, 2021 for Karwaan: The Heritage Exploration Initiative.

Note Accompanying the Performances

The Cursed Land of Lustful Women, a performance by Kanika Gupta Slovene Ethnographic Museum, 15, 17 and 19 August 2021

Fig. 31 : During performance shoot at Tivoli Park, Ljubljana, Slovenia. Credit: Nadja Valentinčič Furlan

Once upon a time in ancient India ...

In ancient India, like in many other ancient cultures, folklore around trees is found in abundance. Human beings relate to nature and have tried to deal with it in different ways. In many cultures people have attempted to live in peace with it, rather than seeing it as an enemy and confronting it. This happened for a very long time, at a time when trees fulfilled all human needs, women were not restrained, when there was no greed. Naturally, trees were the object of worship and ancestors buried under them became spirits of the trees. Yakṣī, was the tree spirit, or the tree deity, a benevolent sorceress, presiding over forests and rivers. And then, social patterns began to change and man began to strive for more of everything, more resources, more power and greed, and more and more greed.

This small performance narrates a folk story which comes from the times when this social and environmental transition was taking place. Though loaded with meaning and symbolism, it is simple in its narrative, a characteristic feature of old myths. The performer, trained in the Indian dance tradition Kathak, derives gestures and movements from that dance form to tell these stories, taking liberty with it and yet going back to the roots of Kathak as a performing arts form, in which the primary agenda was to tell a story.

The performance suggests sentiments without too many words and connects everyday life with nature. The performer attempts to focus on sounds of nature, the wind, trees, the insects and the gentle hum of night, and takes these as music instead of recorded sound. The performance is full of movements done in silence, redolent of sentiment, the juice of aesthetic pleasure.

Who is she? The narrator? The *sūtradhāra* of Nāṭyaśāstra? Is she the princess in the story? Or is she the tree ...

perhaps she was ...

Kanika Gupta: BIO

Kanika Gupta (b. 1987, Delhi) is an art historian, a trained dancer and a filmmaker. She has a Ph.D. from Jawaharlal Nehru University in Delhi on the ancient Indian motif – the female and the tree. She has co-authored a book titled 'Lupadakhe – Unknown Master Sculptors of Ancient India' in 2019, and authored several research papers on Ancient Indian sculpture, aesthetics, painting and mythology. She is a guest faculty at several Universities in India.

The performance is part of a residency program organized by Kanika Gupta within the project Taking Care, Ethnographic and World Cultures Museums as Spaces of Care. The project explores the connections between non-European ethnographic collections and questions regarding the climate crisis and the Anthropocene. (https://takingcareproject.eu/)

Credits

Costume Sourcing:

Sneha Agarwala, Kolkata, West Bengal

Vankar Mukesh, Shilp Art Craft Shop, Bhujodi, Gujarat

Nilesh Shekha, Darshan Handicrafts, Bhujodi, Gujarat

Rehearsal Space Support:

LTG Auditorium, Delhi

Saket's Tango Studio, Saket Prakash, Noida

Slovene Ethnographic Museum, Ljubljana

Candles:

Kavarna SEM lounge bar

Production Support:

Slovene Ethnographic Museum, Ljubljana

Taking Care Project, European Union

Bibliography

Agrawala, Vasudev Sharana. "Kalpavṛkṣa: The Wish Fulfilling Tree" *Journal of the Indian Society of Oriental Art II (1943):1-8.*

Agrawala, Vasudev Sharana. "Yakshas and Nagas." *The Eastern Anthropologist* (1971):1.

Agrawala, Vasudev Sharana. *Ancient India folk cults*. No. 7. Prithvi Prakashan, Vārāṇasi, 1970.

Agrawala, Vasudev Sharana. *Indian Art*. Vishwavidyalya Prakashan, Vārāṇasi, 1965a.

Agrawala, Vasudev Sharana. *Indian Art*. Vishwavidyalya Prakashan, Vārāṇasi, 1965b.

Ahuja, Naman. "The Paradox of International Laws on Preserving and Protecting Heritage". *Art, Politics, Symbols and Religion: A Reader for Humanities and Design Students*. Susan Visvanathan (ed.), Winshield Press. New Delhi, 2019.

Anand S (ed), Ambedkar, Bhimrao Ramji (Author).*Riddles in Hinduism: an exposition to enlighten the masses: The Annotated Critical Selection*. Navayana Press, 2016.

Arya, Meghal. *Spatial Ecology of Water*. AADI Center. Ahemdabad, 2019.

Banerji, Sures Chandra. *A brief history of tantra literature*. Naya Prokash, 1988.

Barrett, Douglas E. *Sculpture from Amravati in the British Museum*. Department of Oriental Antiquities, Trustees of the British Museum, 1954.

Barua, Beni Madhab, *Barhut* Vol.1, 2, 3. Indological Book Corporation, 1937.

Bhattacharya, Bishnupada. *Yāska's Nirukta and the Science of the Etymology. An Historical and Critical Survey.* K. L. Mukhopadhyay. 1958.

Bhattacharyya, Benoytosh. *An Introduction to Buddhist Esoterism.* H. Milford, Oxford University Press, 1932.

Bhattacharyya, Benoytosh. *The Indian Buddhist Iconography.* H. Milford, Oxford University Press, 1924.

Bisht, Ravindra Singh, Silky Agarwal, Mantu Majumder, Amit Prashant. "Archaeological Studies at Dholavira using GPR". *Current Science*, Vol. 114, No. 4, 2018.

Bisht, Ravindra Singh. "Harappa Sabhyata ke Naye Ayam". *Aajkal* Monthly magazine (Hindi), October 1993.

Bisht, Ravindra Singh. *Excavation at Dholavira.* Excavation report to Archaeological Survey of India, 2015.

Bose, Mandakranta. "Dance at the crossroads: An early source of Kathak". *Studies in Hindu and Buddhist Art.* Abhinav Publications. 1999.

Chattopadhyaya, Debiprasad. *Lokāyata A Study in Ancient Indian Materialism.* People's Publishing House, 1959.

Clegg, Margaret. *Human Remains: Curation, Reburial and Repatriation.* University College London, 2020.

Cowell, Edward B. *The Jātaka: Stories of the Buddha's Former Births.* The University Press, 1907.

D.R. Karmarkar (trans). *Abhijñāna-Śākuntala of Kālidāsa.* Chaukhamba Vidya Bhawan.Vārāṇasi, 1952.

DeCaroli, Robert. *Haunting of Buddha: Indian Popular Religions and the formation of Buddhism.* Oxford University Press, 2004.

Devy, N.G. *Indian Literary Criticism,* Theory and Interpretation. Orient BlackSwan, 2010.

Dhavalikar, Madhukar Keshav. "Historical Archaeology in India". *Recent Studies in Indian Archaeology.* Munshiram Manoharlal, 2002.

Dhavalikar, Madhukar Keshav. *Historical Archaeology of India.* Books & Books, 1999.

Dutt, Romesh Chunder. *The Economic History of India*. Publication Division, Ministry of Information & Broadcasting, 1893.

Fergusson, James. *Tree and Serpent Worship*. Cornhill Magazine, 1869.

Forrest, Charles Ramus. *A Picturesque Tour Along the Rivers Ganges and Jumna in India*. London, 1824.

Gokhale, Pradīpa. *Lokāyata/Cārvāka: A Philosophical Inquiry*. Oxford University Press, 2015.

Gopal, Brij, and Malavika Sah. "*Conservation and management of rivers in India: case-study of the river Yamuna.*" Environmental Conservation 20, no. 3, 243-254. Cambridge University Press, 1993.

Gupta, Kanika, "Myth: Methodology and Interpretations" *Folklore Studies in the Current Globalization*, B.R. Publishing Corporation Delhi, 2018.

Gupta, Kanika. *Yakṣī cult in early Mauryan to Kuṣāṇa sculpture*. Unpublished Ph.D. thesis. School of Arts and Aesthetics. Jawaharlal Nehru University. Delhi, 2022.

Gupta, Manjul. *A study of Abhinavabhāratī on Bharata's Nāṭyaśāstra and Avaloka on Dhanañjaya's Daśarūpaka: dramaturgical principles*. Gian Publishing House. New Delhi, 1987.

Habib, Irfan. "Colonialization of the Indian Economy, 1757-1900." *Social Scientist* (1975): 23-53.

Habib, Irfan. *Indian Economy Under Early British Rule, 1757-1857*. Vol. 25. Aligarh Historians Society, 2013.

Habib, Irfan. *Indian Economy, 1858-1914*. Vol. 28. Tulika Books, 2006.

Hindu vratkathayen. Diamond Books, 2006.

Jacobi, Hermann (trans). *Jaina Sutras, Part I, vol* 22. 1884.

Jacobi, Hermann, (trans). *The Kalpasūtra of Bhadrabahu*. 1879.

Jain, Jagdish Chandra. *Jainism and Prakrit in Ancient and Medieval India*. Manohar Publication, 1994.

Jain, Pannalal (ed & tans). *Raviṣeṇāchārya's Padmapurāṇa (Padamacharita) Vol 1, 2 & 3*. (Hindi translation along with original Prākṛt text). Bhartiya Jnanpith. Eighteenth edition, 2017.

Kale, R.M. (trans). *The Mṛichchhakaṭika of Śūdraka*. Motilal Banarsidass Publishers. Delhi, 1924.

Kannal, Deepak, Kanika Gupta. *Lupadakhe:Unknown Master Sculptors of Ancient India.* Mandala Books. 2019.

Kaw, Maharaj Krishen. *Kashmir and it's people: studies in the evolution of Kashmiri society*. Vol. 4. APH Publishing, 2004.

Kher, Geetika. "Subjugation of the Nāgas" *Nirukta*(2006):9-52.

Kosambi, Damodar Dharmanand. *Myth and reality: studies in the formation of Indian culture*. Popular Prakashan, 1962.

Kothari, Sunil. *Kathak: Indian classical dance art*. Abhinav Publications, 1989.

Krishna, T. M. *Reshaping Art*. Aleph, 2018.

Law, BimalaCharan. *The Life and Work of Buddhaghosa*. Calcutta and Simla, Thacker, Spink & Co. 1923.

Levi-Strauss, Claude. *Structural Anthropology*, 1958.

Manna, Ashim. Iñaki Alday, Pankaj Vir Gupta.*Yamuna River Project: New Delhi Urban Ecology*, Actar Publishers, 2018.

Mehendale, M. A. "The Critical Edition of the Mahābhārata: Its Achievement and Limitations." *Annals of the Bhandarkar Oriental Research Institute* 88 (2007): 1-16.

Mehendale, M.A. *Nirukta Notes*. Series II, Deccan College Pune, 1978.

Mehrotra, Arvind Krishna (trans). *The Absent Traveller: Prākrit Love Poetry from the Gāthāptaśatī of Sātavāhna Hāla*. Penguin Books, 2008.

Mirashi V.V, N.R. Navlekar. *Kālidāsa: Date, Life and Works.* Popular Prakashan, 1969.

Moon, Vasant (ed), Ambedkar, Bhimrao Ramji (Author). *Dr. Babasaheb Ambedkar Writings and Speeches* (BAWS). Government of Maharashtra, 1987.

Moro-Abadḻa, Oscar. "The history of archaeology as a 'colonial discourse'." *Bulletin of the History of Archaeology* 16, no. 2 (2006).

Mukherji, Parul Dave. "The Making of Sakuntala: The Erotica and the Paradox of Representation"*Revisiting Abhinanasakuntalam,*

Love, Lineage and Language in Kalidasa's Nataka, Orient BlackSwan, 2011.

Olick, Jeffrey K., Vered Vinitzky-Seroussi, and Daniel Levy (ed). *The collective memory reader*. Oxford University Press, 2011.

Rassool, Ciraj. "Re-storing the skeletons of empire: return, reburial and rehumanisation in Southern Africa." *Journal of Southern African Studies* 41, no. 3, 2015. 653-670.

Ray, Ardhendu. "Iron and the Debate on Second Urbanization". *Heritage: Journal of the Multidisciplinary Studies in Archaeology* 4 (2016): 831-835.

Richman, Paula (ed). *Many Ramayanas: The Diversity of the Narrative Tradition in South Asia.* University of California Press, 1991.

Rowland, Benjamin. *The Art of Central Asia.* The University of California, 1974.

Saini, Anjali, Mamta Chaudhary, Rakhi Solanki. "Survival of Handloom Industry during 19th and early 20th Century in India". *International Journal of trade and Commerce-IIARTC January-June 2015, Vol 4 No. 1.*

Saraswati, K.S. *A Survey of Indian Sculpture.* Munshiram Manoharlal Publishers, 1975.

Sarup, Lakshman. *Yāska. The Nighaṇṭu and the Nirukta: The Oldest Indian Treatise on Etymology, Philology and Sementics*. Critically Edited from Original Manuscripts. Motilal Banarsidass, 1967.

Silvester, Jeremy, Wendy Black, Catherine C. Cole, Winani Therbele, Morongwa N, Mosothwane and Rooksana Omar. "Who were they? Rehumanisation of Human Remains in Museum in Southern Africa". *Museum and Communities: Diversity, Dialogue and Collaboration in an age of Migrations.* Cambridge Scholars Publishing, 2019.

Singh, Kavita. "To Show, To See, To Tell, To Know: Patuas, Bhopas, and Their Audiences." *Picture showmen. Insight into the narrative tradition in Indian art* (1998): 100-115.

Thapar, Romila, "Forest and Settlements" *Environmental Issues in India: A Reader,* Pearson Longman Delhi, 2006.

Thapar, Romila. *Ancient Indian social history: Some interpretations.* Orient Blackswan, 1978.

Trivedi, Madhu. *The emergence of the Hindustani tradition: music, dance, and drama in North India, 13th to 19th centuries*. Three Essays Collective, 2012.

Vatsyayan, Kapila (ed). *Concepts of Space: Ancient and Modern.* Indira Gandhi National Centre for the Arts and Abhinav Publications, 1991.

Vatsyayan, Kapila (ed). *Concepts of Time: Ancient and Modern*. Indira Gandhi National Centre for the Arts, 1996.

Vatsyayan, Kapila. *The square and the circle of the Indian arts*. Abhinav Publications, 1997.

Vázquez, Rolando. "Modernity Coloniality and Visibility: The Politics of Time." *Sociological Research Online* 14, no. 4 (September 2009): 109–15. https://doi.org/10.5153/sro.1990.

Vogel, Jean Philippe. *Indian Serpent-lore: The Nāgas in Hindu Legend and Art*. Asian Educational Services, 1926.

Warikoo, K (ed). *Bamiyan Challenge to World Heritage*. Third Eye and Himalayan Research and Cultural Foundation. Delhi, 2002.

Index

only one ultimate goal of contributing to changing the balance of the sexual division of labour and resources to make it more equitable. This goal applies to various stages of the project cycle. Some others (Macdonald et al., 1997) further argue that once an organisation has accepted a move towards gender sensitivity and gender equality, it should have an array of strategies that it can deploy to carry this aim forward. From the literature, the objectives such as a shift in the gender division of labour, gender parity in staffing at all levels, and making the workplace and work style more women-friendly, and strategies such as gender-sensitive policies (programme, personnel, project etc.) have been found as those that an institution can develop to address the gender needs of both sexes at various levels, institution, project and community. GAD practitioners further argue that gender can be fully imbibed onto the formal agenda of the agencies only by making gender awareness a strategic objective along with a commitment for training on gender analysis to all staff and ensuring adequate resources for gender work.

May (1997) also states that it has become increasingly clear that poverty and social exclusion affect men and women differently, and interventions that do not reflect this difference have in many cases reinforced structural inequalities for women. As Mosse (1993) suggests, if those who plan projects and programmes were better able to understand women's gender interests, they would be in a much better position to ensure that their gender needs are met. In turn, Longwe (1991) recommends three points that the policy-makers need to consider while formulating gender-sensitive plans, programmes and objectives. They are as follows: women have different and special needs, women are a disadvantaged group in terms of their limited access to and control over resources, and women's development entails working towards increased equality and empowerment for women, relative to men. However, if agencies think of benefiting women by using gender-neutral words in their policies, objectives and strategies, and do not necessarily mention women as constituents, they are likely to fail at the objective despite their best intentions. Kabeer (1994a) also argues that the use of gender-neutral terms like 'members', 'communities' etc. in policy documents is usually misinterpreted to benefit only men.

One of the key assumptions underlying a GAD analysis is that women and men, because they have different gender roles and power, also have different gender interests. If the policy-makers understand this reality, they can design objectives that can help to meet the needs of both sexes. However, a review of the objectives and the strategies of NEWAH (1998), RWSSP (1996a & 1996b) and the FRWSSSP/DWSS of the HMG/Nepal (1996a), shows that all these institutions were concerned about meeting only the practical needs of women and men (the need for water) but not women's strategic gender needs. None of the agencies incorporated in their written objectives and strategies that they will aim for a reduction of women's labour, change in women's income, improvement in women's condition, etc. by involving them in the decision-making of project activities and providing them with opportunities to participate in various training programmes, among others. In turn, the project benefits are reaped more by men than women.

> *In RWSSP and FRWSSSP, they mentioned in their strategy that users from the community will form a WUC and the members of the WUC will be provided with the training. Taking undue advantage of these so-called gender-neutral terms, only one woman in the RWSSP and two women in the FRWSSSP were included in the WUC of 11 and 13 members respectively. Accordingly, more men received training in both cases as compared to women. There were many other examples similar to this in which women were deprived of or provided fewer opportunities compared to men - while selecting people for paid and unpaid positions while going on observation tours while giving skill-oriented training etc.*

Amongst the three institutions studied, only the FRWSSSP briefly stated in its objectives that improving the quality of life and the living condition of children, women and men was its goal. However, because the other objectives and strategies of the institution did not coincide with this goal, it could be argued that this goal would only be partially fulfilled as seen in its water project implemented in Hile village.

> *The women in Hile drinking water project (FRWSSSP) had access to safe water near their home, still, there was no change in their quality of life and living conditions as expected. When the water had to be collected from a farther distance, the women were helped by men in this task. However, later, because the water was near the house the men expected more water to be available at home but had completely stopped fetching it. Moreover, due to the unviable location of tap-stands, women were obliged to carry water to their homes to perform their private ablutions, whilst they previously had privacy at the old water sources. This all had meant more burden on women's part (Regmi, 2000).*